Encounters with God

The Book of ROMANS

Encounters with God Study Guide Series

Encounters with God

The Book of ROMANS

Published by Thomas Nelson, Inc., P.O. Box 141000, Nashville, Tennessee 37214.

Scripture quotations are taken from The New King James Version® (NKJV), copyright 1979, 1980, 1982, 1992 Thomas Nelson, Inc., Publishers.

Library of Congress Cataloging-in-Publication Data
ISBN 1-4185-26436

Printed in the United States of America

07 08 09 10 RRD 9 8 7 6 5 4 3 2 1

CONTENTS

Encounters with God

The Book of ROMANS

An Introduction to the Book of Romans

The book of Romans is the first in a series of books in the New Testament called an *epistle*—a formal letter intended to give instruction. This letter was written to a vibrant, growing church in Rome. It is considered one of the greatest documents ever written.

No one knows with certainty how the church was established in Rome. It may have been established by believers who heard Peter's message during the celebration of Pentecost (Acts 2). This church at the heart of the Roman Empire was considered by virtually all in the early church to be in a pivotal, strategic position for influencing Christians throughout Asia Minor and Europe.

In many ways, this letter is more like a theological essay. It makes widespread use of Old Testament Scripture and conveys a deep interest in the role of Judaism. The style of writing is clear and pragmatic. The central theme is *righteousness*—being in right standing with God. The book clearly spells out man's need for salvation and God's righteousness, and it gives doctrinal instruction on how to apply one's salvation in living a righteous life.

About the Author, the apostle Paul. The author of this book, the apostle Paul, was in a unique position to write a theological letter to the believers in Rome. Paul, who received the Jewish name *Saul* at his birth, was born in the Roman city of Tarsus, located in Cilicia. (See Acts 22:3.) A Hebrew by heritage, he grew up in Greek culture. His family members, some of whom appear to have been wealthy and socially influential, were citizens of Rome. Saul received the finest education available and was a strong adherent to the Law of Moses. He became a Pharisee, a leading and powerful sect in Judaism.

He launched vicious attacks against the followers of Christ and was a witness to the deacon Stephen's stoning (Acts 7:58; 8:1). It was while Saul was in zealous pursuit of the followers of *the Way* who had gone to Damascus, intending to persecute them even to the point of death, that he was blinded by a supernatural light and heard the voice of Jesus Christ. (See Acts 9:1–19.) Confronted by Christ Himself, Saul's life was permanently redirected. He became as zealous a messenger for Christ as he had once been a persecutor of Christians. Changing his name to the Greek *Paul*, he proclaimed Christ's good news to the Gentiles with all-consuming passion, and in his lifetime, he launched at least four missionary journeys to spread the message of salvation and reconciliation with God, made possible through Jesus Christ's crucifixion and resurrection.

Paul made no secret of his desire to one day preach the gospel in Rome. Long before that visit became a reality, however, Paul wrote this letter to the Christians there. The letter is dated in the mid-50s AD while Paul was in Corinth. He dictated the letter to a secretary named Tertius (Romans 16:22), shortly before he made a trip to deliver a relief offering from the Gentile churches to the Christians in Jerusalem (Romans 15:25–29). Knowing his trip to Jerusalem would be filled with uncertainties, Paul appears to have dictated this message to the church in Rome to explain why he was delayed in visiting them (Romans 1:1–15), and as a means of preparing the way for his eventual trip there. In the letter, Paul reaffirms he has not abandoned his mission to the Gentiles, nor has he lost confidence in the gospel of Christ for all people. The letter also promotes the need for unity between Jewish and Gentile Christians.

As it turned out, Paul was arrested on false charges during his trip to Jerusalem. He remained in various forms of imprisonment until his case was ultimately appealed to Rome. Several years after writing this letter to the Roman Christians, Paul did arrive in Rome—not as a free-traveling citizen, but as a prisoner under house arrest and awaiting trial. It is highly likely he had contact with members of the church in Rome during his house arrest. There is some evidence to indicate he was released from prison, and then re-arrested at a later time, and he may have had close fellowship with this church during that intermediate time.

The letter to the Romans has been a pivotal book in the history of the church. Several major theologians and preachers through the centuries have cited the book of Romans as being a key factor in either their conversion to Christ Jesus, or to major reforms in their personal ministry that resulted in worldwide impact.

AN OVERVIEW OF OUR STUDY
OF THE BOOK OF ROMANS

This study guide presents seven lessons drawn from and based largely on the book of Romans. The study guide elaborates on, and is based on, the commentary included in the *Blackaby Study Bible*. The lessons are:

Lesson #1: Our Need for Salvation

Lesson #2: The Relationship Between Faith and Works

Lesson #3: Choosing the Call to New Life

Lesson #4: Set Apart for Service by the Holy Spirit

Lesson #5: The Destiny of God's People

Lesson #6: Living with Other Believers

Lesson #7: Living as a Christian in an Ungodly World

Personal or Group Use. These lessons are offered for personal study and reflection or for small-group Bible study. The questions may be answered by an individual reader or used as a foundation for group discussion. A segment titled "Notes to Leaders of Small Groups" is included at the back of this book to help those who might lead a group study of the material.

Before you embark on this study, we encourage you to read in full "How to Study the Bible" in the *Blackaby Study Bible* on pages viii-ix. Our contention is always that the Bible is unique among all literature. It is God's definitive word for humanity. The Bible is

- *inspired*—God breathed

- *authoritative*—absolutely the final word on any spiritual matter

- *the plumb line of truth*—the standard against which all human activity and reasoning must be evaluated

The Bible is fascinating in that it has remarkable diversity, but also remarkable unity. The books were penned by a diverse assortment of authors representing a variety of languages and cultures. The Bible as a whole has a number of literary forms. But, the Bible's message from cover to cover is clear, consistent, and unified.

More than mere words on a page, the Bible is an encounter with God Himself. No book is more critical to your life. The very essence of the Bible is God revealing Himself to mankind.

God speaks by the Holy Spirit through the Bible. He also communicates during your time of prayer, in your life circumstances, and through the church. Read your Bible in an attitude of prayer and allow the Holy Spirit to make you aware of God's activity in and through your personal life. Write down what you learn, meditate on it, and adjust your thoughts, attitudes, and behavior accordingly. Look for ways every day in which the truth of God's Word can be applied to your circumstances and relationships. God is not random, but orderly and intentional in the way He speaks to you.

Be encouraged—the Bible is *not* too difficult for the average person to understand if that person asks the Holy Spirit for help. (Furthermore, not even the most brilliant person can fully understand the Bible apart from the Holy Spirit's help!) God desires for you to know Him and His Word. Everyone who reads the Bible can learn from it. The person who will receive maximum benefit from reading and studying the Bible, however, is the person who:

- *is born again* (John 3:3, 5). Those who are born again and have received the gift of God's Spirit have a distinct advantage in understanding the deeper truths of His Word.

- *has a heart that desires to learn God's truth*. Your attitude greatly influences the outcome of Bible study. Resist the temptation to focus on what others have said about the Bible. Allow the Holy Spirit to guide you as you study God's Word for yourself.

- *has a heart that seeks to obey God*. The Holy Spirit teaches most those who have a desire to apply what they learn. Begin your Bible study with prayer, asking the Holy Spirit to guide your thoughts and to impress on you what is on God's heart. Then, make plans to adjust your life immediately to obey the Lord fully.

As you read and study the Bible, your purpose is not to *create* meaning, but to *discover* the meaning of the text with the Holy Spirit's guidance. Ask yourself, "What did the author have in mind? How was this applied by those who first heard these words?" Especially in your study of the Gospel accounts, pay attention to the words of Jesus that begin "Most assuredly" or "He opened His mouth and taught them, saying." These are core principles and teachings that powerfully impact every person's life.

At times you may find it helpful to consult other passages of the Bible (made available in the center columns in the *Blackaby Study Bible*), or the commentary in the margins of the *Blackaby Study Bible*.

Keep in mind always that Bible study is not primarily an exercise for acquiring information, but it is an opportunity for transformation. Bible study is your opportunity to encounter God and to be changed in His presence. When God speaks to your heart, nothing remains the same. Jesus said, "He who has ears to hear, let him hear" (Matthew 13:9). Choose to have ears that desire to hear!

The B-A-S-I-Cs of Each Study in This Guide. Each lesson in this study guide has five segments, using the word BASIC as an acronym. The word BASIC does not allude to elementary or simple, but rather, to *foundational*. These studies extend the concepts that are part of the *Blackaby Study Bible* commentary and are focused on key aspects of what it means to be a Christ-follower in today's world. The BASIC acronym stands for:

B = Bible Focus. This segment presents the central passage for the lesson and a general explanation that covers the central theme or concern.

A = Application for Today. This segment has a story or illustration related to modern-day times, with questions that link the Bible text to today's issues, problems, and concerns.

S = Supplementary Scriptures to Consider. In this segment, other Bible verses related to the general theme of the lesson are explored.

I = Introspection and Implications. In this segment, questions are asked that lead to deeper reflection about one's personal faith journey and life experiences.

C = Communicating the Good News. This segment presents challenging questions aimed at ways in which the truth of the lesson might be lived out and shared with others (either to win the lost or build up the church).

LESSON #1

OUR NEED FOR SALVATION

Sin: a breach in a person's relationship with God as the result of disobedience to God's commands. Righteousness: being in right-standing with God. Salvation: the bridge between man's sinful state and God's perfection, made possible by the sacrificial death of Jesus Christ on the cross.

B
Bible Focus

> *For I am not ashamed of the gospel of Christ, for it is the power of God to salvation for everyone who believes, for the Jew first and also for the Greek. For in it the righteousness of God is revealed from faith to faith; as it is written, "The just shall live by faith" (Romans 1:16–17).*

> *Do you despise the riches of His goodness, forbearance, and longsuffering, not knowing that the goodness of God leads you to repentance? But in accordance with your hardness and your impenitent heart you are treasuring up for yourself wrath in the day of wrath and revelation of the righteous judgment of God, who "will render to each one according to his deeds": eternal life to those who by patient continuance in doing good seek for glory, honor, and immortality; but to those who are self-seeking and do not obey the truth, but obey unrighteousness—indignation and wrath, tribulation and anguish, on every soul of man who does evil, of the Jew first and also of the Greek; but glory, honor, and peace to everyone who works what is good, to the Jew first and also to the Greek. For there is no partiality with God. For as many as have sinned without law will also perish without law, and as many as have sinned in the law will be judged by the law (for not the hearers of the law are just in the sight of God, but the doers of the law will be justified; for when Gentiles, who do not have the law, by nature do the things in the law, these, although not having the law, are a law to themselves, who show the work of the law written in their hearts, their conscience also bearing witness, and between themselves their thoughts accusing or else excusing them) in the day when God will judge the secrets of men by Jesus Christ, according to my gospel (Romans 2:4–16).*

> *But now the righteousness of God apart from the law is revealed, being witnessed by the Law and the Prophets, even the righteousness of God, through faith in Jesus Christ, to all and on all who believe. For there is no difference; for all have sinned and fall short of the glory of God, being justified freely by His grace through the redemption that is in Christ Jesus, whom God set forth as a propitiation by His blood, through faith, to demonstrate His righteousness, because in His forbearance God had passed over the sins that were previ-*

ously committed, to demonstrate at the present time His
righteousness, that He might be just and the justifier of the
one who has faith in Jesus" (Romans 3:21–26).

Paul makes it very clear in writing to the Romans that the same rules apply
to everyone. God doesn't play favorites! No one is exempt from the need for
salvation. And no one—on the basis of their previous religious background,
culture, nationality, or socioeconomic status—will be denied salvation if that
person truly believes in Jesus Christ and accepts the reconciliation with God
the Father that Jesus has made possible.

This is good news! Your ability to have a fully reconciled relationship with
God does not depend on any factor related to *your birth*. Rather, your salvation
is totally related to all factors corresponding to *Christ's death and subsequent
resurrection*. Everyone enters into a reconciled relationship with God the
Father through the same door labeled *salvation*. The key to that door is *faith*,
or belief.

Paul was writing to two groups of Christians in the church at Rome.

First, there were the Jews, who grew up keeping the Law of Moses, but who
had become followers of Jesus. Paul told them, "Don't think that because you
have been saved by faith, you are freed from all constraints related to repen-
tance. You are freed from sin's binding constraints so that you might freely live
a life in full accordance with the Law. You have not been freed to live a life
apart from the definitions of godly behavior spelled out by the Law. You must
have *patient 'continuance in doing good.'*" (See Romans 2:7.)

In today's age, some people have grown up in very strict or traditional
denominations or even pagan religions. They accept Jesus as Savior and feel
such spiritual freedom in their new relationship with God the Father they
believe they are freed of all restraints. Not so! Paul's message to them would
be the same as to the Jews who found Christ in Rome—God requires a godly
life. Paul makes it very clear that *glory, honor, and peace* are to everyone who
works what is good, and *indignation and wrath, tribulation and anguish* are to
everyone who does evil (Romans 2:8,10). God's standards regarding right
behavior haven't changed!

Also in the church at Rome were Gentiles who had not grown up with the
Law and who basically had led *lawless* lives. To these believers, Paul writes
that in many ways, the law rooted in a person's conscience is as exacting as
the Law of Moses. Nevertheless, their salvation is not a result of their *good
deeds* or *good nature*. They, too, needed to receive Jesus Christ as Savior to be
in right relationship with God.

Neither keeping the Law, nor doing good deeds as a good person, produces
salvation. Salvation *only* comes by belief in Jesus Christ as God's Son and
mankind's Savior.

In turn, salvation does not give license to lay aside the Law, to think any person in any position is above the Law, or to dismiss one's conscience. Rather, Jesus Christ empowers His followers to live a godly life.

No matter who you are, you need what Jesus came to give. You need to be saved.

No matter your background, you are called to receive God's offer of salvation made possible through the shed blood of Jesus. God's offer of salvation is freely given to all people.

No matter how you grew up, you are called to live a life marked by good deeds. Your salvation makes it possible for you truly to live a godly life.

When it comes to the nature of sin, the means of salvation, and the fruit of salvation born out in godly behavior, God's definitions and protocols are the same for all people.

Do you think if you keep the rules of your church you are in right relationship with God? No.

Do you think by being a *good* person you are in right relationship with God? No.

Do you think because you are a believer in Jesus, you can live however you like? No.

The key to being saved is believing in Jesus Christ and placing your total trust in Him as your Savior.

The key to living a godly life is trusting Jesus as your Savior to free you completely from the grip of sin.

This is what it means to be *saved*.

A
Application for Today

Four funerals were scheduled at the Evergreen Funeral Home. At the first funeral, the preacher said about the deceased, "He was a good man. He was a good son to his parents, a good husband to his wife, a good father to his children. He was honest and paid his taxes, never broke the law even to the point that he never had a parking ticket, and he always gave a contribution to the poor at Christmas. He never missed voting in an election. He was a good businessman who treated his employees fairly. He helped build a playground in the park for our town's children. May he enjoy a good reward in heaven."

At the second funeral, the preacher said about the deceased, "She was a good woman who loved her family and her friends. She was the kind of woman people call a 'pillar of the church.' She participated in the women's club and made quilts for the missionaries. She sang in the choir for twenty years and always baked wonderful pies and cakes for the annual church bazaar to raise money for the homeless. She went to Bible studies and hardly ever missed attending church. She even participated in door-to-door evangelism missions to invite people to church. She made sure her children went to Sunday school, church, and youth group. May she enjoy rest from all her labors in heaven."

At the third funeral, the preacher said about the deceased, "I don't know very much about this woman, but I know she was baptized as a baby at the church I pastor, and that she went through confirmation class when she was twelve. We know she is in heaven today with her parents and grandparents who helped build the church where they were all members."

At the fourth funeral, the preacher said about the deceased, "He had a tough life and made lots of mistakes. In fact, he hurt a few people very badly and he lived with guilt about what he had done. But a few years ago, this man came to my office and told me he wanted to get things right with God. He fell on his knees that afternoon and we prayed together as he confessed to God he had sinned, told God he believed Jesus was the Son of God and the Savior he needed, and asked God to forgive him of his sins. After that day, he began to come to church and sat quietly in the back pew on most Sundays. I know a number of you here today are people with whom he talked privately about his new relationship with Jesus, and about the peace he had found for his soul. I have heard from several people since he died about how he came to you to try to make things right and to heal the hurts he had caused. We can rejoice today without any doubt that this man is with Jesus in heaven."

What is your response to each of these eulogies? What would you have said about each of these people?

S
Supplementary Scriptures to Consider

Many people today are concerned about the eternal fate of those who have never heard the gospel. They do not believe God plays fair with all people—allowing some to hear the gospel and others to live and die without ever hearing the name of Jesus. Paul wrote to the Romans that God has given to every person a witness about Himself:

> For the wrath of God is revealed from heaven against all ungodliness and unrighteousness of men, who suppress the truth in unrighteousness, because what may be known of God is manifest in them, for God has shown it to them. For since the creation of the world His invisible attributes are clearly seen, being understood by the things that are made, even His eternal power and Godhead, so that they are without excuse, because, although they knew God, they did not glorify Him as

God, nor were thankful, but became futile in their thoughts,
and their foolish hearts were darkened. Professing to be wise,
they became fools, and changed the glory of the incorruptible
God into an image made like corruptible man—and birds and
four-footed animals and creeping things.

Therefore God also gave them up to uncleanness, in the
lusts of their hearts, to dishonor their bodies among themselves, who exchanged the truth of God for the lie, and
worshiped and served the creature rather than the Creator, who
is blessed forever. Amen" (Romans 1:18–25).

• In what ways is it possible to see and understand God through the *things
that are made*? (Romans 1:20). What is a person led to conclude if he
sees the glory and power of God in creation and compares it to his own
flawed nature and limited ability? When a person sees himself as being
finite and flawed in the presence of an infinite and perfect God, what
keeps that person from crying out to God for mercy and help?

• What response does Paul believe all who recognize and know God should
make toward Him?

• What does it mean to you to *exchange the truth of God for the lie* (Romans 1:25)?

• What does it mean for a person to have *worshiped and served the creature rather than the Creator* (Romans 1:25)?

• God is both just and merciful. Many people do not like the truth that at times God manifests wrath against ungodliness and unrighteousness. What do you say to someone who wants only a peaceful, loving, merciful God who never moves against evil? If there is no justice for the unrighteous, can there be justice for the righteous?

Many people contend it is possible to be a *good* person—one who never does anything overtly evil from birth until death—and those who are *good* (according to the standards of their respective culture or religion), do not need to accept Jesus as their Savior. Here is what Paul wrote to the Romans:

> For we have previously charged both Jews and Greeks that they are all under sin.

As it is written:
"There is none righteous, no, not one;
There is none who understands;
There is none who seeks after God.
They have all turned aside;
They have together become unprofitable;
There is none who does good, no, not one."
"Their throat is an open tomb;
With their tongues they have practiced deceit";
"The poison of asps is under their lips";
"Whose mouth is full of cursing and bitterness."
"Their feet are swift to shed blood;
Destruction and misery are in their ways;
And the way of peace they have not known."
"There is no fear of God before their eyes"
(Romans 3:9–18). See also Psalms 5:9; 10:7; 13:1–3; 36:1;
53:1–3; 140:3; Ecclesiastes 7:20; Isaiah 59:7–8.)

• Are we ever fully capable of judging the inner thoughts, motives, and desires of others?

• What does this passage—based on several Old Testament passages—say about unredeemed, unregenerated human nature?

• Is there any sin you would be incapable of committing if you did not have the help of Christ Jesus to live a godly life? On what basis do you believe you would have human power or ability to withstand that temptation to sin?

I
Introspection and Implications

1. Is there anything you no longer believe you need to do to live a godly life now that you have accepted Jesus as your Savior? On what basis do you believe you are free from that former rule, ritual, or tradition?

2. Do you believe there are different gradations of sin—all the way from dastardly evil to only-a-little-less-than-perfect? On what basis do you hold that belief?

3. In what ways do you believe all people are equal before God? Consider these statements and add others of your own. Ask yourself about each statement: On what do I base my belief?

• All people are born as sinners and remain as sinners until they accept Jesus as their Savior.

• All people need to be saved.

• God has made a way for all people to know Him.

• God has made the way to salvation freely available to all who will believe in Jesus as the Christ.

• God has called all people to come into right relationship with Him.

• God desires for all people to live godly lives.

• God automatically saves every person He creates.

C
Communicating the Good News

What does it do to a person's motivation to witness about Jesus as being the Son of God, and the sacrifice for all sin, if that person does not believe everyone is in need of a Savior?

Do you agree or disagree with the following statement, and why?

"What we believe about salvation determines what we do about evangelism—about sharing the gospel with other people."

LESSON #2

THE RELATIONSHIP BETWEEN FAITH AND WORKS

Faith: belief
Works: behavior

B
Bible Focus

> *Where is boasting then? It is excluded. By what law? Of*
> *works? No, but by the law of faith. Therefore we conclude that*
> *a man is justified by faith apart from the deeds of the law*
> *(Romans 3:27–28).*

> *What then shall we say that Abraham our father has found*
> *according to the flesh? For if Abraham was justified by works,*
> *he has something to boast about, but not before God. For what*
> *does the Scripture say? "Abraham believed God, and it was*
> *accounted to him for righteousness" (Romans 4:1–3; see also*
> *Genesis 15:6).*

> *For the promise that he would be the heir of the world was*
> *not to Abraham or to his seed through the law, but through the*
> *righteousness of faith. For if those who are of the law are*
> *heirs, faith is made void and the promise made of no effect,*
> *because the law brings about wrath. . . . Therefore it is of faith*
> *that it might be according to grace, so that the promise might*
> *be sure to all the seed, not only to those who are of the law,*
> *but also to those who are of the faith of Abraham, who is the*
> *father of us all (Romans 4:13–14,16).*

From cover to cover, the Bible's message is clear: People come into relationship with God the Father through believing.

This Bible truth, however, is a major point of contention or confusion for many people, for several key reasons.

For some, faith seems too simple or too easy. They ask, "How can believing alone bring a person into a right relationship with God the Father?" From their perspective, the gap between finite, flawed man and perfect, glorious, infinite God seems too great to be bridged by belief alone. Surely, they conclude, the formation of a bridge between God and man must require something more difficult, more demanding.

For others, faith seems too vague. They want verifiable evidence, a checklist of deeds, a ladder of accomplishment. They want to know where they are on the journey from sinner to forgiven child of God. They seek benchmarks of progress.

For some, faith seems too fluctuating and unsteady. They tend to ask, even subconsciously: "Does great faith one day mean a closer relationship with God and wavering faith the next day mean a person is in danger of slipping out of

God's everlasting arms?" "Is it possible to lose faith?" "Is it possible to fall out of relationship with God once a relationship has been established?"

As we approach God's Word, we must always remember this: We don't get to make up the rules or set the protocol. We don't get to pick and choose the concepts, principles, or commandments we like, and discard the rest—as if we are filling our plates from the dishes on a buffet table. God gave His commandments. He provided the method by which all men must be saved. God sent His Son to provide salvation through the atoning sacrifice He paid when he died in our place. We have only one real choice: to obey God and do things His way, or to disobey God and do things our own way. In the end, the ultimate obedience is to *believe* God is, that God's way is the only way, and to believe Jesus is the Savior. It is in our believing that God establishes a fully reconciled relationship with us, empowers us with His Spirit, and enables us to walk in a way that is pleasing to Him.

Have you ever believed in Jesus and experienced His salvation?

Do you find it difficult simply to believe and be saved? Why?

Do you rejoice that this is all that is required?

You may be thinking, *But what about works?* Behavior automatically flows from belief. Behavior manifests or displays belief to the outside world.

Our behavior is never the means of salvation. Behavior is never a substitute for belief. In other words, behavior does not produce or give rise to belief. Rather, belief produces and gives rise to behavior.

God intends for the two to work together. It may be helpful to think of it this way: Belief is the root and behavior is the fruit that it bears.

At the core of both belief and behavior is a person's will. We *choose* to believe as an act of our will. We then choose to *behave* as an act of our will. When the two are in accord—a perfect alignment of belief and behavior—we have integrity as followers of Christ Jesus.

Do you find it easier to *behave* than to *believe*? Or, do you find it easier to *believe* than to *behave*?

To what degree does your life display true integrity (a clear alignment between belief and behavior)?

A
Application for Today

Megan was a doer. She served on every church committee possible and was the first to volunteer when a call went out to polish the church pews, deliver food to a grieving family, or take flowers from the bouquet on the church altar to a church member in the hospital. People often said about Megan, "What a godly woman she is!" What people didn't know was that Megan was *not* motivated to do her good deeds by genuine love for God, but out of fear that if she did not produce enough good works, God might, in her words, "send her to hell." Her fear of God included a fear of her mother, who not only had taught her to fear God but also had taught her never to disappoint the family. Megan lived in fear that if she didn't do enough for the church, her mother might rise from her grave and reprimand her, or at the very least, Megan's failure to perform to the utmost of all expectations might tarnish the family's reputation. Her mother, after all, had been the president of the women's society. Megan's good works masked bad theology and a genuine lack of faith in a loving, faithful, forgiving God.

How could you ever discover Megan's hidden turmoil? What would you say to her? Or, would you remain silent if you suspected Megan's inner pain, but did not want to offend her?

Bill, Megan's husband, didn't go to church. He had stated forcefully on several occasions, "I believe in Jesus and that's enough." He often went to his office or puttered in his workshop on Sunday mornings. He did not keep Megan from her church work, nor did he prohibit her from giving financially to the church, but he refused to attend church functions with her. Bill's refusal to become involved in the church was not an act of stubborn defiance, as many of Megan's friends assumed. Bill had been deeply wounded by things *church people* had said about him and his family while growing up. He genuinely believed Jesus was the Savior and he often sneaked a peek in the Bible he kept in his desk drawer at work. Bill's fears of rejection or ridicule were just as great as Megan's fears of failure or criticism. They shackled him from displaying his faith in practical ways.

How would you discover Bill's hidden turmoil? What would you say to him? Or, would you also remain silent if you suspected Bill's inner pain, for fear of offending him?

S
Supplementary Scriptures to Consider

Jesus not only spoke truth. He fulfilled the truth of what He taught and said by His deeds, both His miracles of healing and deliverance, and ultimately, His death on the cross.

> As through one man's offense judgment came to all men, resulting in condemnation, even so through one Man's righteous act the free gift came to all men, resulting in justification of life. For as by one man's disobedience many were made sinners, so also by one Man's obedience many will be made righteous (Romans 5:18–19).

• In what ways is believing an act of obedience?

• In what ways is behavior required if we truly seek to obey God?

• What difference would it have made if Jesus had taught, healed, and delivered as He did, but had *not* died on the cross?

• Based on your behavior, what do people conclude about your beliefs?

All behavior has consequences—not only physical, but in relationships, in reputation, and in spiritual reward.

> For the wages of sin is death, but the gift of God is eternal life in Christ Jesus our Lord (Romans 6:23).

• Can you cite an example in which sin killed a relationship? Caused disease that led to death? Destroyed a person's reputation or opportunity for influence?

• How does a person behave if he receives an extremely valuable gift? Is it ever considered sufficient only to believe in response to a valuable gift, but not express that attitude or opinion in words and deeds?

Nothing we do can *save* us, apart from placing our trust in Jesus Christ as our Savior.

> For by grace you have been saved through faith, and that not of yourselves; it is the gift of God, not of works, lest anyone should boast (Ephesians 2:8–9).

Even the faith we have is *not of ourselves; it is the gift of God* (Ephesians 2:8). The exercise of our faith is what brings us into right relationship with God, and it is also a factor in our behavior.

Faith enables us to believe in God and to believe in Jesus as our atoning sacrifice for sin.

In what ways does faith also impact our behavior?

How does faith help us in our responses to difficult situations or in our dealing with a difficult person?

Does it take faith to give generously?

Does it take faith to act and then trust God with the ultimate success of your good deeds? Cite specific examples.

I
Introspection and Implications

1. In your experience, how have faith and works blended together? Do you have difficulty expressing your faith in words or deeds?

2. Can you cite an example of someone who modeled faith plus works for you in a positive manner?

3. In what ways have you sought to teach your children—or others in the next generation with whom you have contact—the balance of faith and works?

4. What happens if faith doesn't produce godly works?

5. What happens if good works aren't rooted in faith?

6. Is there a difference between good works and godly works?

C
Communicating the Good News

The Jewish understanding of *works* includes the words we say. Every statement a person utters is considered a deed; an act reflecting belief; a bit of work that requires a person's energy, skill, and time; and that which produces a result of some kind. Who spoke to you about Jesus Christ?

In what ways is your relationship with the Lord today a result of the words others spoke into your life?

In what ways is it important that good *words* be joined with good *works* as part of our witness about Christ?

LESSON #3

CHOOSING THE CALL TO NEW LIFE

Election: God choosing us
Adoption: God making us His beloved children

B
Bible Focus

> *For as many as are led by the Spirit, these are sons of God. For you did not receive the spirit of bondage again to fear, but you received the Spirit of adoption by whom we cry out, "Abba, Father." The Spirit Himself bears witness with our spirit that we are children of God, and if children, then heirs—heirs of God and joint heirs with Christ, if indeed we suffer with Him, that we may also be glorified together (Romans 8:14–17).*

> *The righteousness of faith speaks in this way. . . "The word is near you, in your mouth and in your heart" (that is, the word of faith which we preach): that if you confess with your mouth the Lord Jesus and believe in your heart that God has raised Him from the dead, you will be saved. For with the heart one believes unto righteousness, and with the mouth confession is made unto salvation. For the Scripture says, "Whoever believes on Him will not be put to shame." For there is no distinction between Jew and Greek, for the same Lord over all is rich to all who call upon Him. For "whoever calls on the name of the LORD shall be saved" (Romans 10:6,8–13).*

> *We know that all things work together for good to those who love God, to those who are the called according to His purpose. For whom He foreknew He also predestined to be conformed to the image of His Son, that He might be the firstborn among many brethren. Moreover whom He predestined, these He also called; whom He called, these He also justified; and whom He justified, these He also glorified (Romans 8:28–30).*

Did you choose God? Or, did God choose you?

Does a person truly have free will to chart his course through life? Or, does God ultimately map out every human life? Do we have little recourse but to eventually comply with what has been pre-designed?

These questions have been at the heart of many philosophical musings and discussions through the ages. In Romans 8 Paul addresses the matter in a very straightforward manner:

You are chosen by a loving God—just as a parent chooses a child for adoption. But at some point, it is incumbent upon you, as a child, to choose to be a full participant in the adoption. You must choose to be chosen, and live accordingly.

Remember the apostle Paul is writing, in part, to Jews. As a people, they had believed for thousands of years they were the chosen people of God. The Gentiles had no concept of being chosen by God, but they did understand the concept of being adopted. Adoption was a common practice in Rome, with adopted sons legally granted certain rights that were greater than those rights given to the naturally-born children of a father. Paul writes that both Jews and Gentiles had been chosen by God, but the child is required to choose to enter into and exercise the full rights associated with being a son or daughter of the Most High.

Today, the secular concept of universalism teaches that every person is automatically redeemed by God on the basis of their having been created by God. The apostle Paul states very clearly that salvation occurs when a person believes in his heart and confesses that Jesus is Savior. There is nothing *automatic* about salvation. While God's desire is for every person to say "yes" to His call, and while He is ardent and relentless in His pursuit of each person, in the end, a person can choose to reject God and His plan of salvation, even as a person must choose to accept God's way to be saved.

In like manner, God created each person with a specific plan and purpose in mind. He endowed each person with certain talents and placed each person in a specific environment of opportunity and challenge so those talents might be developed and used for godly service. God does not force compliance with His plan and purpose, however. He allows us to choose to embrace what he has done on our behalf and to choose to walk fully in the path He has set before us. It is up to us, however, to choose God's way, and to continue to choose God's way day after day, each step of the journey.

Also in like manner, God desires for each person to receive Christ and to grow to maturity as a Christian. He does not, however, force us to conform to Christ. Once again, we must choose what God has chosen for us. As we do, God refines, justifies, and glorifies us in His timing and by His methods.

Have you said "yes" to His plan of salvation?

Have you chosen what God has chosen for you?

Have you said "yes" to the unique life He has given you? How are you developing them and using your life for godly purposes?

Have you said "yes" to the Spirit, and are you growing up into the fullness of Christ's character as you allow the Spirit to work in you and through you?

Of one thing we can always be certain: God's way is for our eternal benefit. His plan for us is the one that will ultimately be the most fulfilling, satisfying, and joyful for us to follow.

A
Application for Today

Have you ever known a child—perhaps an adult child—who chose to disown his or her parents, or one parent in particular? It happens, and increasingly so, it seems, in this age when divorce is so rampant in our society. Sadly, it happens in the church as well. In many cases, a child distances himself from the relationship because of past abuse, including what the child perceives to be emotional abuse. In some cases, the child distances himself because he feels abandoned or rejected by the parent. Disowning the parent gives the child a sense of equal authority in the relationship.

One person explained why she had distanced herself from her father. "It's a simple case of tit for tat—He left me when I was seven, so I leave him now." In some cases, the child simply doesn't know how to relate to the parent, or is rarely around the parent. Perhaps the child feels communicating with the *bad* parent is a matter of disloyalty to their *good* parent, or simply doesn't seek to communicate with the parent for any number of reasons, some of which may be sheer negligence. In these cases the relationship is simply neglected and as a result, withers.

Regardless of the reason for the disowning or distancing behavior, the net result is the same: estrangement, hurt, and loss. Who experiences the most loss? In most cases, it is the child, and eventually, the child's children. No person is one hundred percent correct or loving at all times, but rarely is any person one hundred percent in error, evil, or unloving. A wise child sees a parent and regards that relationship realistically, and reaches out in love and compassion to do his or her best to heal a broken relationship. Rather than disown, a child is wise to seek to reclaim, with God's help, any degree of relationship that might be possible.

What about those who disown a relationship with God the Father? Sometimes people have a faulty perception of God—they see Him as all justice and no mercy, all punishment and no love. Sometimes people feel God hasn't played fair with them or done things their way or to their liking. Although these descriptions of God are not true, sin distorts reality and causes an untrue perception of who God really is. As a result, some people acknowledge God, but simply neglect pursuing a relationship with Him. The end result is also estrangement, hurt, and loss. And who loses the most? The child.

God the Father is reaching down, His everlasting arms open wide. What can be said to a child who folds his arms and refuses to be picked up and held in a loving embrace?

S
Supplementary Scriptures to Consider

As believers in Christ Jesus, we are invited to call God *Abba*—an affectionate reference to His Fatherhood, similar to calling God *Daddy*.

> The Spirit Himself bears witness with our spirit that we are children of God, and if children, then heirs—heirs of God and joint heirs with Christ, if indeed we suffer with Him, that we may also be glorified together (Romans 8:16–17).

• What does it mean to you to be an heir of God? A joint heir with Christ?

• What do you say to the person who says all people are *children* of God?

• Is suffering a part of being a joint heir with Christ? (Are there forms of suffering that are not physical or torturous?)

• What does it mean to be glorified together with Christ?

Is it possible to condemn yourself by sheer failure to accept Christ? Recall the words of Jesus to Nicodemus:

> "For God did not send His Son into the world to condemn the world, but that the world through Him might be saved.
> "He who believes in Him is not condemned; but he who does not believe is condemned already, because he has not believed in the name of the only begotten Son of God. And this is the condemnation, that the light has come into the world, and men loved darkness rather than light, because their deeds were evil. For everyone practicing evil hates the light and does not come to the light, lest his deeds should be exposed. But he who does the truth comes to the light, that his deeds may be clearly seen, that they have been done in God" (John 3:17–21).

• What does the phrase *loved darkness rather than light* (John 3:19) mean to you? Why do we instinctively attempt to hide when we do something we know is wrong?

• What connections do you see between this passage from the Gospel of John and the story of Adam and Eve in Genesis 3, especially their attempt to hide *themselves from the presence of the* LORD *God among the trees of the garden* (Genesis 3:8)?

• What are the benefits of choosing Jesus as our Light?

• What are the benefits of choosing the light of truth that the Holy Spirit seeks to impart to us?

The presentation of the gospel of Jesus Christ calls to people in a special way to choose what God has prepared for them:

> We are bound to give thanks to God always for you, brethren beloved by the Lord, because God from the beginning chose you for salvation through sanctification by the Spirit and belief in the truth, to which He called you by our gospel, for the obtaining of the glory of our Lord Jesus Christ (2 Thessalonians 2:13–14).

• Consider a mother who chooses to prepare a delicious meal for her children and then calls to them from the front porch to come in from their outdoor activities to eat supper. In what ways is this an appropriate metaphor for God's choosing and calling us?

• What links do you see in your own life between being chosen and called?

The Scriptures point to specific blessings that belong to the believer, and to the church as a collective body of believers. Paul wrote:

> What then shall we say to these things? If God is for us, who can be against us? He who did not spare His own Son, but delivered Him up for us all, how shall He not with Him also freely give us all things? Who shall bring a charge against God's elect? It is God who justifies. Who is he who condemns? It is Christ who died, and furthermore is also risen, who is even at the right hand of God, who also makes intercession for us. Who shall separate us from the love of Christ? Shall tribulation, or distress, or persecution, or famine, or nakedness, or peril, or sword? As it is written:
> "For Your sake we are killed all day long;
> We are accounted as sheep for the slaughter."
> Yet in all these things we are more than conquerors through Him who loved us. For I am persuaded that neither death nor life, nor angels nor principalities nor powers, nor things present nor things to come, nor height nor depth, nor any other

created thing, shall be able to separate us from the love of God which is in Christ Jesus our Lord (Romans 8:31–39).

• What does it mean to know Christians are more than conquerors (Romans 8:37)?

• What does it mean to know Christ *makes intercession* for you (Romans 8:34)?

• In what ways do people sometimes struggle with the concept that nothing separates the church from the love of Christ?

I
Introspection and Implications

1. Are you emotionally comfortable with the concept that God is *Abba*—your loving heavenly Father? How has your relationship with your earthly father affected your understanding of God and your relationship with Him?

2. We stated in an earlier study that God does not play favorites when it comes to making an offer of salvation. Yet, God does have a special relationship with those who accept Jesus as their Savior and seek to follow Him as their Lord. What specific benefits do you see as belonging to the believer (and not to the unbeliever)? Have you fully chosen to receive those benefits and live in the truth of them?

C
Communicating the Good News

Do you believe God truly desires for *all* people to know Him and come into relationship with Him through Jesus Christ? In what ways does your answer define what you believe about soul-winning or evangelism?

Lesson #4

SET APART FOR SERVICE BY THE HOLY SPIRIT

Sanctification: the process of God purifying His children so they might be set aside for holy service.

B
Bible Focus

> *I beseech you therefore, brethren, by the mercies of God,*
> *that you present your bodies a living sacrifice, holy, accept-*
> *able to God, which is your reasonable service. And do not be*
> *conformed to this world, but be transformed by the renewing*
> *of your mind, that you may prove what is that good and*
> *acceptable and perfect will of God (Romans 12:1–2).*

Few people have ever said more in fewer words than the apostle Paul in these two verses from the book of Romans.

There are at least eight concepts that deserve our careful consideration.

I beseech you therefore, brethren. Paul is imploring his brothers and sisters in Christ. His tone is one of urgency and earnest desire for the believers in Rome to act diligently and immediately on his words.

Note especially the word *therefore.* It refers to the verse immediately preceding this passage:

> *For of Him and through Him and to Him are all things, to*
> *whom be glory forever. Amen (Romans 11:36).*

God is Creator of all. He is the arranger and orchestrator of His creation, always in control of all things at all times. He works in and through human lives. And He alone is worthy of all praise, honor, and glory. As Jesus taught His disciples to pray, "Yours is the kingdom and the power and the glory forever" (Matthew 6:13).

Present your bodies a living sacrifice. Sacrifices in the Old Testament were poured out, burned up, or waved before the Lord. Jesus, and none of the New Testament writers, advocated a continuation of those sacrifices, but the parallels of these three forms of sacrifice are part of Christian worship: we are to *pour out our love* in worship to God and in practical service to others at all times and in all ways possible. We are to *give our energy, skills, and talents* in worship to God and service to others, in a way that is all-encompassing and all-consuming, and to become martyrs if that is required. We are to *offer praise and thanksgiving* to the Lord continually as we serve God and others. It is in these ways that we are *living* sacrifices.

Holy, acceptable to God. To be holy means literally to be *set apart.* In order for God to accept an offering in the Old Testament, it had to be pure and without blemish. This was true also for the vessels used in the worship rituals of the tabernacle and temple. We are to set apart our lives—keep ourselves pure and invite the refining and purifying work of the Holy Spirit—so God can use us on a moment's notice in any situation.

Reasonable service. The apostle Paul sees this as *reasonable* since Christ Jesus presented Himself in this manner for our salvation. Because all things are *from* God and are *owing to* God, it only stands to reason that *all* our lives should bear His mark and be offered to Him.

This phrase has also been translated *spiritual worship.* The concept of worship is *service* rendered unto the Lord.

Do not be conformed to this world. The world has systems and protocols rooted in power, fame, and human fleshly desires. Paul writes that the world's systems are not what God has designed for the church.

Transformed by the renewing of your mind. Truly to grasp what Paul has written about God *(for of Him and through Him and to Him are all things)* and what he has challenged the believers to do *(present your bodies a living sacrifice)* requires a change in perspective, attitude, and thinking. It requires *transformation*—a re-creating of the old to produce total newness. Before we can truly *be* a living sacrifice we must see things as God sees them. We must be able to feel His heartbeat for the world, hear His voice clearly, and understand what He requires and desires for us. This new way of thinking is made possible only through the power of the Holy Spirit. We must yield ourselves continually to the Holy Spirit, inviting Him to create us anew into the likeness of Christ Jesus.

You may prove what is *that good and acceptable and perfect will of God.* To prove, in this case, is to live out the will of God in practical, everyday situations and circumstances. It is to test out God's will and design in our mundane experiences and human relationships. We are to become living examples of God's *goodness*—a testament to His love, mercy, forgiveness, and ongoing blessings. We are to display behaviors completely *acceptable* to God—a breathing, living example that it is possible to obey God's commandments. We are to live *whole* or *perfected* lives—without separation or disharmony; but rather, a life of wholeness in body, soul, spirit, and relationships.

What a tall order this is! What a challenge God has given to us! And here is the good news:

By the mercies of God. We are not able to present ourselves to the Lord as a living sacrifice by our own initiative or behavior. We are only able to do this because of the mercies of God. It is the Holy Spirit who cleanses us and renews us and calls us to holy service.

As we present ourselves, willingly submitting all areas of our lives to the Lord, He renews us. *Our* part is to yield our lives to Him. *His* part is to perfect us and use us.

Spend time reflecting on these verses from Romans.

Is serving God your foremost priority and desire?

What is God requiring of you?

In what ways does He desire for you to prove that His will for you is rooted in what is *good and acceptable and perfect?*

In what ways are you trusting the Holy Spirit for His help and leading?

A
Application for Today

"The problem with making my life a living sacrifice," a man once said with a very loud sigh, "is that it requires *everything* I have and am."

He was correct. God desires we hold nothing back from Him.

List several roles you currently fill. For example, spouse, parent, worker, neighbor, citizen, church member. What does God require of you in each of these areas of your life?

God has given to you time, talent, and resources. What does He require of you when it comes to your use of time, the employment of your talent, and the giving of your resources?

God has called us to spiritual disciplines, including praise and thanksgiving, intercession, and study of His Word. What does God require of you when it comes to the time you spend in these disciplines?

Too often we overlook the rewards of sacrifice. God *always* receives, multiplies, and returns to us what we sow to Him. If pain or suffering is involved in sacrifice, we can count on the return we will receive to be one of overflowing blessing, reward, joy, satisfaction, and fulfillment.

Pause to consider the truth that God has given to you far more than you have ever sacrificed or will ever sacrifice to Him.

S
Supplementary Scriptures to Consider

What is the nature of the sacrifice God desires of us? Read what the psalmist said:

> O Lord, open my lips,
> And my mouth shall show forth Your praise.
> For You do not desire sacrifice, or else I would give it;
> You do not delight in burnt offering.
> The sacrifices of God are a broken spirit,
> A broken and a contrite heart—
> These, O God, You will not despise (Psalm 51:15–17).

• What does it mean to have a *broken spirit*? (Consider the spirit of the unsaved person is rooted in pride, lust, and greed.)

• What does it mean to have a *broken and a contrite heart*?

• In what ways are we *each* called to sacrifice our pride and desires?

The psalmist also had this to say about sacrifice:

I will offer to You the sacrifice of thanksgiving,
And I will call upon the name of the LORD (Psalm 116:17).

- What does it mean to you to *offer . . . the sacrifice of thanksgiving*?

- In what ways does *thanksgiving* require that we take no personal credit for what we have acquired or become?

Sacrifice is costly. Sacrificial giving involves generosity in giving something we value or prize. In seeking to acquire the threshing floor of Araunah to build an altar to the LORD, King David said this:

> "I will surely buy it from you for a price; nor will I offer burnt offerings to the LORD my God with that which costs me nothing." So David bought the threshing floor and the oxen for fifty shekels of silver. And David built there an altar to the LORD, and offered burnt offerings and peace offerings. So the LORD heeded the prayers for the land, and the plague was withdrawn from Israel (2 Samuel 24:24–25).

• What is it you value most in life? (Consider your time, relationships, possessions, those things that make your life comfortable. What do you least desire to do without?)

• In what ways does giving something you value highly take on the quality of sacrifice?

• What rewards were associated with David's sacrifice?

• What rewards do you believe God may give to you as you offer your life as a living sacrifice to Him?

• What danger is there in sacrificing to get a reward?

I
Introspection and Implications

1. What is the foremost emotion you associate with sacrifice?

2. In what ways does the concept of sacrifice force us to deal directly with our own pride?

3. Do you truly desire to be set apart for holy service? Why or why not? What is the Lord speaking to your own heart?

4. In what ways is the Lord challenging you *not* to conform to this world, but to be *transformed* into the likeness of Christ Jesus?

C

Communicating the Good News

Jesus sacrificed *all* so we might have eternal life and forgiveness of sins. What are you willing to sacrifice so another person might hear the gospel and have an opportunity to receive Jesus as Savior?

Are you part of a church that believes and practices

- the sacrifice of praise and thanksgiving?

- sacrificial giving to win the lost to Christ Jesus?

- the sacrifices associated with holy living—acceptable living before God?

LESSON #5

THE DESTINY OF GOD'S PEOPLE

Destiny: the purpose God designed for your life
and the life of all who are in His body

B
Bible Focus

> *There is therefore now no condemnation to those who are in Christ Jesus, who do not walk according to the flesh, but according to the Spirit. For the law of the Spirit of life in Christ Jesus has made me free from the law of sin and death (Romans 8:1–2).*

> *I consider that the sufferings of this present time are not worthy to be compared with the glory which shall be revealed in us. For the earnest expectation of the creation eagerly waits for the revealing of the sons of God. For the creation was subjected to futility, not willingly, but because of Him who subjected it in hope; because the creation itself also will be delivered from the bondage of corruption into the glorious liberty of the children of God. For we know that the whole creation groans and labors with birth pangs together until now. Not only that, but we also who have the firstfruits of the Spirit, even we ourselves groan within ourselves, eagerly waiting for the adoption, the redemption of our body. For we are saved in this hope, but hope that is seen is not hope; for why does one still hope for what he sees? But if we hope for what we do not see, we eagerly wait for it with perseverance (Romans 8:18–25).*

Two words sum up Paul's description of the destiny God has purposed for His people: *freedom* and *fulfillment*.

Freedom. To be free is to walk unshackled by an ever-present impulse to sin. It is to live without the oppression of guilt or the dark cloud of shame. It is to live apart from continually demanding lusts of the flesh, the lust of the eyes (greed), and the pride of life. To be free is to have the privilege to say "yes" to the Lord's opportunities without any hesitation. To be free is to experience the empowerment of the Holy Spirit to resist all temptations, to pursue all truth, and to engage fully in loving and godly relationships with other people.

Very specifically we have been set free of

- *all condemnation* (Romans 8:1). No accusation from the devil about our relationship with God is valid. As Christians, we are now fully defined by what God says about us, not what the devil might whisper in our ear.

- *the law of sin and death* (Romans 8:2). This law says unforgiven sin functions as a seed of death in us—it produces a harvest of decay and destruction. The book of Romans is a clear statement that when God forgives sin, He removes all consequence of spiritual death associated with it. This does not mean a person may not need to pay for his sin during this life. Someone who commits murder, for example, may need to pay for that sin with life in prison or even death. But, it does mean a person will not need to pay for his sin *after* death. Even the most vile criminal can rest assured of eternal life if he receives Jesus as his Savior. Christ's sacrifice on the cross allows us to be forgiven and to receive eternal life after death, regardless of the enormity or extent of our past sin.

Throughout Paul's letters, we read of the freedom we have to become a slave to Christ—to make the choice to serve Christ at all times, in all situations and relationships, and in all places.

Fulfillment. To be *fulfilled* means to experience a deep and abiding satisfaction in life—to know joy, meaning, and purpose without measure. It is to be content in life and trust that you are in the hands of almighty God.

What a life God holds out to those who will trust Him and obey Him in all things! Truly, as Paul says, *the sufferings of this present time are not worthy to be compared with the glory which shall be revealed in us* (Romans 8:18).

At no time in God's Word do we find a promise that the Christian life will be a rose garden without thorns, or a garden without any need of cultivation, pruning, watering, or pest control. To the contrary, God's Word tells us we live in a world that is corrupted, and in which most human endeavors are futile. The good news for the Christian in a bad-news world is that God is with us and He is preparing us for a future in which all that is corrupt will be redeemed, and all that seems futile will be fully rewarded or recompensed.

Neither does the Word of God promise us that either freedom or fulfillment are automatic and quickly received. Not all impulses to sin may be removed from a person's life in the moment of new birth. Life may not take on the glow of full satisfaction and meaning the moment a person confesses his sin and is forgiven. Freedom and fulfillment are both immediate and a processes—irreversible, once a person has been born again. The work of Christ in our life is complete, but we must choose to appropriate all that He has done. Our life becomes the sum total of the choices we make in our relationship with Christ. But there will come a day when all of His purposes in our life are fulfilled and we know absolute freedom and fulfillment. We can *count* on that day coming!

In what ways do you still struggle with feeling fully free from all lusts of the flesh, lusts of the eyes, and the pride of life?

In what ways are you stronger today in resisting temptation than you were when you first accepted Jesus as your Savior?

In what ways must you continue to trust the Holy Spirit to set you free in every area of your life?

In what ways are you experiencing more and more fulfillment in your life as you follow Jesus as your Lord?

In what ways do you trust the Holy Spirit daily to give your life meaning and deep satisfaction?

A
Application for Today

"I'm just a housewife and a mom," Steffie said. "I spend my days chasing a three-year-old, doing laundry, and fixing dinner."

"What a wonderful life you have," her sister Lyssa said. "I spend my days getting coffee for my boss, typing memos, answering the phone, and filing."

"I envy you both," Vince said, wading into the conversation with his two sisters. "I'm outside in all kinds of weather clearing roads of ice and snow, and then fixing potholes afterward."

None of these three siblings saw themselves as either *free* or *fulfilled*. They felt trapped by their circumstances. Then they went to visit their cousin Dave, who had returned from the war without the use of his legs and missing one arm. He had recently been released from the hospital but was still in daily rehabilitation.

"Man, this is tough," Vince said to his cousin, taking Dave's one available hand with a firm grasp.

"I have a great life!" Dave replied. The cousins looked a little skeptical. "No, I'm not just saying that," Dave continued. "I can't do much yet, but I figured there was one thing I had plenty of time to do and that was to pray. I spend a lot of time every day just thanking God and praising Him—you know, there are hundreds of things to be thankful for every day. I pray for my family—including you three—and my doctors and nurses and physical therapists, and the guy building my prosthetic arm, and my buddies still overseas. I listen to audio tapes of the Bible and Bible teachings—I've learned more about the Bible in the last three months than I ever knew before. I have an opportunity every day to talk about God with other people at the rehab center, and last week I was able to pray with a guy to accept Christ. I'm getting really good at one-handed typing on the computer and I think there may be a job for me in customer service using the phone and computer."

"Don't you feel trapped?" Steffie asked.

"Nope," Dave said, "Feeling trapped has nothing to do with this chair or being in a bed." He tapped the side of his head with his fingers and added, "Feeling trapped is in here. It's a matter of how you think."

"Don't you feel cheated that this happened to you?" Lyssa asked.

"No," Dave said. "I made a choice to serve my country through the military. Now I need to make a new choice about how I am going to serve other people."

Dave was free of bitterness and resentment, and thus, was able to see his circumstances as an opportunity to serve God. In serving God, he found fulfillment and purpose.

In what ways did Steffie, Lyssa, and Vince need to change their perspective, and lay aside bitterness and resentment associated with their daily chores and responsibilities?

In what ways might these three cousins see their respective situations as offering them tremendous freedom to serve God?

When we feel free to serve others, and actually engage in that service, don't we always find fulfillment?

S
Supplementary Scriptures to Consider

Paul taught the Roman Christians that their destiny was tied to their continued belief in the goodness of God. He reminded them they had been *grafted* into the rich faith of the Jewish people, but that not all Jews had remained true to that faith. Some had become more aligned with secular society than with the people of God:

> Because of unbelief they were broken off, and you stand
> by faith. Do not be haughty, but fear. For if God did not
> spare the natural branches, He may not spare you either.
> Consider the goodness and severity of God: on those who
> fell, severity; but toward you, goodness, if you continue
> in His goodness. Otherwise you also will be cut off. And
> they also, if they do not continue in unbelief, will be
> grafted in, for God is able to graft them in again. For if
> you were cut out of the olive tree which is wild by nature,
> and were grafted contrary to nature into a cultivated
> olive tree, how much more will these, who are natural
> branches, be grafted into their own olive tree? (Romans
> 11:20–24).

• What does it mean to you to *continue in His goodness* (Romans 11:22)? Cite practical examples.

• What emotions tend to take root in a person who no longer sees God's goodness at work in all things?

• In what ways do we sometimes cut ourselves off from God's presence and blessings?

• What attitudes tend to take root in our lives when we lose our sense of awe *(fear)* at God's redemptive work and begin to think we are self-sufficient in all things, including our own spiritual growth?

Who knows your personal destiny better than you do? The apostle Paul wrote:

> Likewise the Spirit also helps in our weaknesses. For we do not know what we should pray for as we ought, but the Spirit Himself makes intercession for us with groanings which cannot be uttered. Now He who searches the hearts knows what the mind of the Spirit is, because He makes intercession for the saints according to the will of God (Romans 8:26–27).

• When you don't know what direction to take, or what the will of God might be for your life, what do you do?

- In what ways do we experience weakness when we do not discern God's will?

I
Introspection and Implications

1. Hope is believing the future God has for you is better than anything in your past. It is confident expectation that everything God promised, He will do. Do you live in hope and expectation today? Why or why not? How can you rekindle your hope?

2. To what extent do we sometimes condemn ourselves? How does self-condemnation keep a person from experiencing genuine inner freedom?

3. How *free* do you feel today? To what degree is your sense of freedom a spiritual matter more than a matter rooted in outward circumstances?

4. How *fulfilled* do you feel today? Are you content in the life situation God has placed you? Is feeling fulfilled always ultimately a spiritual matter?

C
Communicating the Good News

Many times those who are newly born again seem to reflect greater spiritual *freedom* than those who have been born again and have served the Lord for many years. Why do you think this is so? How important is it to remind ourselves continually about what God has done for us in redeeming us from sin and leading us into new life?

In what ways do we need to encourage one another to find meaning and purpose in our lives?

LESSON #6

LIVING WITH OTHER BELIEVERS

*Spiritual gifts: abilities that are given by the
Spirit and through which the Spirit works*

B
Bible Focus

> *For I say, through the grace given to me, to everyone who
> is among you, not to think of himself more highly than he
> ought to think, but to think soberly, as God has dealt to each
> one a measure of faith. For as we have many members in one
> body, but all the members do not have the same function, so
> we, being many, are one body in Christ, and individually
> members of one another. Having then gifts differing accord-
> ing to the grace that is given to us, let us use them: if
> prophecy, let us prophesy in proportion to our faith; or
> ministry, let us use it in our ministering; he who teaches, in
> teaching; he who exhorts, in exhortation; he who gives, with
> liberality; he who leads, with diligence; he who shows
> mercy, with cheerfulness (Romans 12:3–8).*

No matter what else a believer may have going for him, he can count on
two things: he has been given a measure of faith, and he has a function to
fulfill in the body of Christ.

We are challenged to grow in both faith and function!

Faith. Jesus chided His disciples on occasion for having *little faith*
(Matthew 8:26; 16:8; Luke 12:28), and marveled on one occasion at the
great faith He saw in a Gentile (Matthew 8:10). Faith, therefore, has degrees,
and the clear understanding of the New Testament writers is that a person
can grow in faith. How? By exercising it—by choosing to trust God and then
seeing God prove Himself utterly trustworthy. Our faith is kindled and
expanded as we apply our faith to life's challenges and see how God acts on
our behalf.

We are to *pray* with faith (James 1:6–8 and 5:15), *live* by faith (Romans
1:17), and *walk* by faith (2 Corinthians 5:7). To whatever degree we can
believe, we are to infuse our daily activities with that degree of belief. Jesus
said, "Did I not say to you that if you would believe you would see the glory
of God?" (John 11:40).

Function. When it comes to our role in church, the apostle Paul taught the
believers in Rome they each had been given distinct and individualized gifts,
but with the overall purpose that these gifts work together. The gifting of the
Holy Spirit was not for them to use as they saw fit, but was for an assignment given by God. No gift is regarded as more important than any other
gift. All gifts are to be evident in the church. Every gift imparted to a per-

son—whether natural or spiritual—was to be used in service to build up the whole of the body of Christ.

Paul wrote specifically that the gifts *"differ according to the grace that is given to us"* (Romans 12:6). It is the Holy Spirit who imparts, enables, and empowers the gifts, and directs the use of the gifts. We do not choose our gifts, any more than we choose our eye color. We can develop and grow in the gifts that have been given to us, but we cannot impart a gift to ourselves.

Certainly not everyone who has the gift of prophecy—or of ministry, teaching, exhortation, giving, leading, or showing of mercy—will manifest that gift in exactly the same way. Our unique personalities, prior experiences, cultural influences, and natural talents and abilities are also called into play. One may prophesy, which is to speak God's Word through song, dramatic story-telling, preaching, or in private counseling sessions. All are valuable expressions of prophecy. In like manner, one may teach or exhort using a variety of methods. One may give any number of things in varying amounts and degrees—including time, talent, money, and other resources—to a wide variety of areas within the church. There are many ways of administering and styles of leadership, and countless ways of showing mercy to others. The central focus of all ministry, however, is God's Word. The Holy Spirit does not inspire, empower, or bless anything that is not in direct agreement with the principles of God's Word. The Holy Spirit is not our servant, but equips us to obey the Lord and to do His will.

"In proportion to our faith (Romans 12:6). Although this phrase is specifically applied to prophecy in this passage of Scripture, the concept is applicable to our employment of all gifts. As a person grows in faith, he experiences an expanded ability to minister! Growing faith produces growing ministries, including greater boldness, enlarged vision, and greater motivation to help others and trust God with the results.

Again, the good news for each of us is that God has given us a role to fulfill and faith with which to believe in Him as we fulfill that role. He has a place for each person to serve within His body, and He challenges us to occupy that place to the full extent of His ability through the Holy Spirit, which is appropriated by our faith.

What level of faith do you have today? In what ways is God challenging you to use your faith, and to grow in faith?

Do you know the assignment God has for you in the body? Have you recognized the gifts the Spirit has given you to fulfill that assignment? Are you growing in your use of those gifts? Are you expressing those gifts actively and continually in the body of Christ? In what ways is God challenging you to trust Him for greater impact in your ministry?

A
Application for Today

"How big is God?" Emmie, age three, asked in all sincerity.

"What a great question!" Aunt Jill replied. Eager to explore her little niece's understanding of God, she then asked, "How big do *you* think God is?"

Emmie said with great resolution and assurance, "I think He's big enough."

Aunt Jill was a bit surprised at such wisdom. "Big enough for what?" she asked. Emmie smiled and said, "God is big enough for everything."

As Emmie got up and headed out the door to explore the garden outside, Jill reflected on what her niece had said. Earlier in the day, she and her niece had been singing together, "He's got the whole world in His hands . . . He's got you and me, brother, in His hands . . . He's got the whole world in His hands." Jill smiled and said to herself, "Emmie got the message."

But then, Jill began to wonder if *she* had the message.

Did she see God as bigger than her problems at work? Than her neighbor's arthritis? Than her brother's doubt? Than her failed romantic relationship? Than the challenges she was facing in leading the children's choir at church?

It's not the size of the problem, Jill mused, *but how big we see God as being. Truly, God is bigger than any problem. He is big enough to handle anything.*

Growing in faith is very often a simple matter of growing in our ability to see that God is big enough to handle the problem that besets us. The bigger the problem, the greater our need to see God as being bigger still!

What problem are you facing today?

Do you believe in a God who is big enough to handle it?

S
Supplementary Scriptures to Consider

The apostle Paul gave very practical advice in how believers were to treat one another:

> Let love be without hypocrisy. Abhor what is evil. Cling to what is good. Be kindly affectionate to one another with brotherly love, in honor giving preference to one another; not lagging in diligence, fervent in spirit, serving the Lord; rejoicing in hope, patient in tribulation, continuing steadfastly in prayer; distributing to the needs of the saints, given to hospitality (Romans 12:9–13).

• What does it mean to you for love to be *"without hypocrisy"* (Romans 12:9)?

• What challenges do we face in abhorring evil, yet not rejecting the person who displays evil behavior?

• How important is it to *"cling to what is good"* (Romans 12:9)? What are the challenges we face in first defining what is *good*?

• What challenges does a person face *"in honor giving preference to one another"*(Romans 12:10)?

- Consider each of the attributes of behavior in this passage. Is one attribute more difficult or problematic for you? Why? What do you believe God is leading you to do about it?

Paul admonished the believers in Rome to edify one another—to build up one another for mutual good by calling them to moral excellence and obedience to God's commands:

> We then who are strong ought to bear with the scruples of the weak, and not to please ourselves. Let each of us please his neighbor for his good, leading to edification. For even Christ did not please Himself; but as it is written, "The reproaches of those who reproached You fell on Me." For whatever things were written before were written for our learning, that we through the patience and comfort of the Scriptures might have hope. Now may the God of patience and comfort grant you to be like-minded toward one another, according to Christ Jesus, that you may with one mind and one mouth glorify the God and Father of our Lord Jesus Christ (Romans 15:1–6).

- What is the fine line between admonishing a fellow believer who is in error and seeking to *"please his neighbor for his good"* (Romans 15:2)? In what ways might we help a person by emphasizing and applauding the good we see, and de-emphasizing our focus on the bad?

• How do we maintain patience with a person who seems to be slow to grow in the Lord? Is our impatience with a person really impatience with God to work within that person?

• What does it mean to be joined with others to have *"one mind and one mouth"* to *"glorify the God and Father of our Lord Jesus Christ"* (Romans 15:6)? How does group praise and thanksgiving focus us collectively on those things that produce a church-wide benefit?

In the passage that follows, the apostle Paul made it clear that our role with other believers is to help, not hinder, a person's spiritual growth:

> We shall all stand before the judgment seat of Christ. For it is written:
> "As I live, says the LORD,
> Every knee shall bow to Me,
> And every tongue shall confess to God."
> So then each of us shall give account of himself to God.
> Therefore let us not judge one another anymore, but rather resolve this, not to put a stumbling block or a cause to fall in our brother's way (Romans 14:10–13).

• What does it mean to put a *stumbling block* in another believer's way? Have you ever experienced this in your life? What were the results?

• The great equalizer for all believers—mature and immature—is that we all must give account for our *own* behavior and we all must bow to Christ one day. How difficult is it, however, *not* to judge others, or to compare ourselves to others?

The mutual love, acceptance, and edification Paul advocated was balanced by a clear recognition that divisions and offenses should not be overlooked or tolerated:

> Note those who cause divisions and offenses, contrary to the doctrine which you learned, and avoid them. For those who are such do not serve our Lord Jesus Christ, but their own belly, and by smooth words and flattering speech deceive the hearts of the simple (Romans 16:17–18).

• According to Paul, what are the motives of those who cause division in the church? How can we identify those who have wrong motives, yet appear, at least superficially, to be doing good works?

• What are the tactics that "dividers" tend to use? How can we avoid falling victim to these tactics?

In many ways, our greatest ministry in the church is often one of *presence*—of simply *being* with a person in their good and bad times:

> Rejoice with those who rejoice, and weep with those who weep. Be of the same mind toward one another. Do not set your mind on high things, but associate with the humble. Do not be wise in your own opinion (Romans 12:15–16).

• What does it mean not to be *wise in your own opinion*? How critical is it to know the Word of God to be wise in it?

• What is the difference between having godly ambition and setting your mind *on high things*?

• What does it mean to *be of the same mind toward one another*?

I
Introspection and Implications

1. Respond to this question: Is it more important to be in agreement with another person regarding what is right in God's eyes, or to be right in your opinionated argument with another person? Why?

2. What do you face as your biggest challenge in getting along with the most problematic person in your church? How would the apostle Paul instruct you in this matter?

3. What is the biggest challenge you are presently facing as you seek to fulfill God's assignment for you within the church? Have you based your service upon your ability or upon the gifts of the Holy Spirit? What would the apostle Paul say to encourage you as you struggle with this challenge? What instruction would the apostle Paul give you?

C
Communicating the Good News

Every person desires to be part of a group where he or she is known, acknowledged as valuable, and is invited to participate fully.

- What challenges do you face in making every new believer, or new visitor to your church, feel welcome?

• What challenges do you face as a church in getting to know new members and valuing their giftedness?

• What challenges do you face as a church in giving new believers an opportunity to serve the body of Christ according to their "measure of faith" (Romans 12:3)?

Lesson #7

LIVING AS A CHRISTIAN IN AN UNGODLY WORLD

Ungodly: not devoted to or obeying God

B
Bible Focus

Owe no one anything except to love one another, for he who loves another has fulfilled the law. For the commandments, "You shall not commit adultery," "You shall not murder," "You shall not steal," "You shall not bear false witness," "You shall not covet," and if there is any other commandment, are all summed up in this saying, namely, "You shall love your neighbor as yourself." Love does no harm to a neighbor; therefore love is the fulfillment of the law.

And do this, knowing the time, that now it is high time to awake out of sleep; for now our salvation is nearer than when we first believed. The night is far spent, the day is at hand. Therefore let us cast off the works of darkness, and let us put on the armor of light. Let us walk properly, as in the day, not in revelry and drunkenness, not in lewdness and lust, not in strife and envy. But put on the Lord Jesus Christ, and make no provision for the flesh, to fulfill its lusts (Romans 13:8–14).

The greatest witness to the indwelling Spirit of Christ Jesus is a godly life. The world hears what we say, but even more so, it watches how we live as Christians. Far more than desiring to see us fail, many of those people in the world who are without Christ desire to see a life that has integrity—a life in which belief, words, and deeds are in perfect alignment. In the long run, integrity *always* wins.

The apostle Paul clearly states in writing to the church in Rome that if we love others as Christ loved us, we will have a desire to keep the commandments and they will no longer be a burden to us (Romans 13:11–14). The cure for every temptation is increasing obedience to God. The more we love and obey God, the more we will chose the best for others. Those who lust do not truly face a lust problem, but are challenged in this area with maturity. When one is not yet strong enough to resist sexual temptation, she or he may involve others in sexual sin. Those who covet have a faith problem. They lack the faith to know that God loves them enough to provide everything that they need. Therefore, they do not have to covet what others have.

We are wise to pray for compassion, for empathy, and for a growing desire to see others come to Christ and grow in Him. The world may rail against God's commandments and standards of justice, but the world inevitably yields to godly mercy and love.

Paul wrote to the believers in Rome that they were to *put on the armor of light* (Romans 13:12). What a wonderful metaphor this is! We are to live without guile, hidden motives, backroom alliances, or secret sins. Our greatest defense as we walk through a world bound in sin is to live without anything to hide and nothing that needs to be covered up. Those who are bound in sin are shrouded by guilt and shame. They usually find themselves irresistibly drawn to people who openly profess God's power of forgiveness and who live without besetting guilt. They often say, "I want the peace, joy, confidence, and sense of purpose you seem to have."

Paul also very specifically called on the believers in Rome to shun revelry, drunkenness, lewdness, lust, strife, and envy. He was describing Roman culture, the very atmosphere and debauchery of ancient Rome. Just as the believers were called to abstain completely from the ways of the world evident all around them, so believers today are called to abstain from anything in their culture not in full accord with God's commandments. To abstain from ungodly behavior was—and still is—to put on Christ (see Romans 13:14).

How difficult do you find it to abstain from ungodly behavior? What is the source of our ability to resist the temptation to engage in the cultural evil of our day? A greater awareness of God's great love for us!

How difficult do you find it to love others to the point of not sinning against them? What is the source of your ability to keep God's commandments? A greater awareness of God's love for others!

Again and again, we are called back to a central truth of the book of Romans: If we truly believe in God and have accepted Jesus as our Savior, we will want to love others as Christ loved us, and do good to others even as God does good to us. We will want to abstain from evil, and pursue what is godly.

A
Application for Today

The two travelers were eating lunch in quiet conversation at a YWCA hostel in Europe. They had decided to stay as guests at this particular hostel for three months, making it their headquarters as they explored the surrounding countryside and cities. They had been at the hostel for two weeks when they were approached by two young women who were living as permanent residents at the "Y" while they started their careers in that particular city.

"You're Christians," one of the young residents said as she sat down at their table. She wasn't asking a question, but making a statement.

"Yes," said one of the travelers a bit hesitantly.

"We could tell," said the other young woman.

"How?" asked the other traveler.

"We've been watching you. You don't swear, you go out on Sunday mornings and come back after lunch which means you are probably going to church, and you don't tell dirty stories. You are nice to all the women here at the hostel, even those from other nations and races."

"But mostly," said the other girl, "you treat each other with kindness. You do good things for each other. And you bow your heads and say a little prayer before you eat your meals."

"Are you Christians?" one of the travelers asked.

"We try to be," said one of the young women. "But you are better Christians than we are. Will you teach a Bible study for us?"

A ministry was birthed in that hour.

Do people know you are a Christian without ever talking to you? Do they see you as a living letter of God's love? Do they want to be more like you in character?

S
Supplementary Scriptures to Consider

Preaching is central to the service that Christians render to the unsaved world. Preaching, of course, is not exclusive to those who are ordained clergy. Every Christian is called to preach to those he or she encounters in the daily course of life. Preaching is proclaiming the good news of Jesus Christ and declaring the sovereignty of God. The will of God is that the gospel be preached far and wide:

> How then shall they call on Him in whom they have not believed? And how shall they believe in Him of whom they have not heard? And how shall they hear without a preacher? And how shall they preach unless they are sent? As it is written:
> > "How beautiful are the feet of those who preach the gospel of peace,
> > Who bring glad tidings of good things!"
> But they have not all obeyed the gospel. For Isaiah says, "LORD, who has believed our report?" So then faith comes by hearing, and hearing by the word of God (Romans 10:14–17).

- What are some practical ways someone might speak the Word of God in day-to-day living as they go about their chores and fulfill their responsibilities?

- In what ways does hearing the Word of God activate your faith?

Central to our role as Christians is that we be agents of peace in our world. "Let us pursue the things which make for peace and the things by which one may edify another" (Romans 14:19).

- What are the things you believe might *make for peace* in your current and most difficult or demanding life situations?

• The word *edify* means to help another person improve their
morals or knowledge of godly behavior. How do you edify others
in your workplace? Family settings? Your children's sporting
events? In your neighborhood? In your church? Do these ways
differ according to whether you are dealing with fellow Christians
or with unbelievers? Do they differ according to whether the
environment is public or private?

The apostle Paul gave specific instructions on how we are to treat those who
do *not* treat us well:

1. Bless those who persecute you; bless and do not curse
   (Romans 12:14).
2. Repay no one evil for evil. Have regard for good things in
   the sight of all men. If it is possible, as much as depends
   on you, live peaceably with all men. Beloved, do not
   avenge yourselves, but rather give place to wrath; for it is
   written, "Vengeance is Mine, I will repay," says the Lord.
   Therefore,
      "If your enemy is hungry, feed him;
      If he is thirsty, give him a drink;
      For in so doing you will heap coals of fire on his head."
      Do not be overcome by evil, but overcome evil with
   good (Romans 12:17–21).

• How important is it to break a cycle of vengeance to establish
peace?

• Cite a specific example in which you experienced good overcoming evil.

• Practically speaking, what does it mean for you to *bless those who persecute you* (Romans 12:14)?

• What does it mean to *have regard for good things in the sight of all men* (Romans 12:17)?

• What is the difference between standing up for what is right and fighting against those who are wrong?

- The admonition to *bless those who persecute you; bless and do not curse* (Romans 12:14) is in the midst of Paul's teachings about how believers are to treat one another. Is it possible for people in the church to persecute one another? What challenges do we face in blessing those who may curse us, even those who call themselves Christians?

I
Introspection and Implications

1. Do unbelievers identify you as a Christian by your behavior? How do you know they consider you to be a believer in Christ Jesus?

2. Respond to this statement: Sometimes it seems easier to love a sinner than to love a fellow believer.

3. Who is it the Lord may be convicting you to love *more*? How might you express your love in a godly manner?

C
Communicating the Good News

When the world looks at your church, what does it see? What top five descriptive words or phrases do you believe an unsaved person might use to describe your church?

NOTES TO LEADERS
OF SMALL GROUPS

A s the leader of a small discussion group, think of yourself as a facilitator
with three main roles:

- Get the discussion started

- Involve every person in the group

- Encourage an open, candid discussion that remains focused on the Bible

You certainly don't need to be the person with all the answers! In truth,
much of your role is to ask questions, such as:

- What impacted you most in this lesson?

- What part of the lesson did you find troubling?

- What part of the lesson was encouraging or insightful?

- What part of the lesson would you like to explore further?

Express to the group at the outset of your study that your goal as a group is
to gain new insights into God's Word—this is not the forum for defending a
point of doctrine or a theological opinion. Stay focused on what God's Word
says and means. The purpose of the study is also to share insights of how to
apply God's Word to everyday life. *Every* person in the group can and should

contribute—the collective wisdom that flows from Bible-focused discussion is often very rich and deep.

Seek to create an environment in which every member of the group feels free to ask questions of other members to gain greater understanding. Encourage group members to voice their appreciation to one another for new insights gained, and to be supportive of one another personally. Take the lead in doing this. Genuinely appreciate and value the contributions each person makes.

You may want to begin each study by having one or more members of the group read through the section provided under "Bible Focus." Ask the group specifically if it desires to discuss any of the questions under the "Application for Today" section, the "Supplemental Scriptures to Consider" section, and the "Introspection and Implications" and "Communicating the Good News" section. You do not need to come to a definitive conclusion or consensus about any question asked in this study. Rather, encourage your group if it does not have a satisfactory Bible-based answer to a question that the group engage in further asking, seeking, and knocking strategies to discover the answers! Remember the words of Jesus: "Ask, and it will be given to you; seek, and you will find; knock, and it will be opened to you. For everyone who asks receives, and he who seeks finds, and to him who knocks it will be opened" (Matthew 7:7–8).

Finally, open and close your study with prayer. Ask the Holy Spirit, whom Jesus called the Spirit of Truth, to guide your discussion and to reveal what is of eternal benefit to you individually and as a group. As you close your time together, ask the Holy Spirit to seal to your remembrance what you have read and studied, and to show you ways in the upcoming days, weeks, and months how to apply what you have studied to your daily life and relationships.

General Themes for the Lessons

Each lesson in this study has one or more core themes. Continually pull the group back to these themes. You can do this by asking simple questions, such as, "How does that relate to _____?" "How does that help us better understand the concept of _____?" "In what ways does that help us apply the principle of _____?"

A summary of general themes or concepts in each lesson follows:

Lesson #1
OUR NEED FOR SALVATION
Every person's need for salvation
The call to live a righteous, godly life
Good living compared to godly living

Lesson #2

THE RELATIONSHIP BETWEEN FAITH AND WORKS

The link between belief and behavior

Lesson #3

CHOOSING THE CALL TO NEW LIFE

Free will

Being adopted by God the Father

Being *called* compared to being *chosen*

Lesson #4

SET APART FOR SERVICE BY THE HOLY SPIRIT

Sacrificial living

Holy living

Not being conformed to the world

Spiritual transformation and the renewal of the mind

Lesson #5

THE DESTINY OF GOD'S PEOPLE

Freedom from condemnation

Freedom from the law of sin and death

Fulfillment in life

Lesson #6

LIVING WITH OTHER BELIEVERS

Holy Spirit equips for ministry

Believing in the greatness and goodness of God

Edification of fellow believers

Unity within the body of Christ

Lesson #7

LIVING AS A CHRISTIAN IN AN UNGODLY WORLD

Standards of godly behavior

Integrity—alignment of belief, words, and deeds

NOTES

NOTES

NOTES

LaVergne, TN USA
03 November 2009
162884LV00003B/9/P